Right Around the Wight

Anne Holley

Published by New Generation Publishing in 2023

First Edition

ISBN: 978-1-80369-952-3

www.newgeneration-publishing.com

New Generation Publishing

Dedication

I dedicate my book to my best friend Janet.

Over many years she has been my rock and I have been hers.

Through highs and lows, laughter and tears

and of course Prosecco.

Acknowledgements

A big thank you to Felicity Fair Thompson for all her help, support, and words of wisdom, guiding me through to get my book finished.

To Andrea Emblin for her lovely drawings, bringing my story together.

To Katie Mansbridge who encouraged me to write an account about my walk 13 years ago, enabling me to refer back and write my book.

John Waterman for his patience when I throw a wobbly at my laptop and 'just can't do' and also for his support.

RIGHT AROUND THE WIGHT

I decided that I needed a new challenge so drumming my fingers on the coffee table I ran through a few options. Sky dive, no, climb a mountain, no, and so on and so on.

I put it to my friends, that proved very helpful, potholing, no, deep sea diving, no, eat creepy crawlies (only a dish full Rosie) yuck. I am calling these people my friends!!

Going to bed that night very frustrated that no one could come up with anything, I wasn't going to give up, another day tomorrow, another day to think.

Pitch dark still, eyes wide open 'that's it' my love of walking, being fit, well sort of, certainly my love of the island, I shall walk around the Isle of Wight in one hit. Crikey, think straight Rosie, well I am, 3 o'clock in the morning is always a good time for me. Come on, pen and paper at the ready, write down some notes and ideas.

After about an hour I was ready for more sleep, my mind had calmed down enough to drift off for a few hours. This has always proved successful in the past, if my mind gets clogged up and I wake in the night, pen and paper is always at the ready. In fact, I have pen and paper in every room, loo as well, just in case a thought comes into my mind that might be useful (you may laugh) but at my age it is very necessary. Otherwise a good idea can be lost forever.

Feeling very excited I start broadcasting to all and sundry 'this is my challenge'. Of course lots of questions from everyone, when, why, how far is it, hmm, that's a point, methinks, a very, very, long way!!!

Going through my list of things to do, yes set a date, mid summer, yes, I think the weekend of the 18th/19th July, start praying now Rosie for a fine weekend.

Along with organizing my challenge, I decided to get going with filling my pot for my charity the Earl Mountbatten Hospice. A hairdresser by trade, a few haircuts here and there, whether my friends wanted a short back and sides, I didn't ask!! My love of gardening, do some grass cutting and weeding. A job that I really, really love doing, being on the end of a pressure hose. My friends Carol and Ted desperately needed their paving power washed, so, decked up from head to foot in my waterproofs and wellies….. me going great guns on the pressure hose, Ted sweeping with much enthusiasm, our task was in full force. Two minutes later I was leaping around the garden like someone possessed, a broom handle in my eye, hmm, a tad uncomfortable, such were our antics. Carol was laughing uncontrollably, Ted absolutely mortified. Once my pain had subsided, checking to see if I still had an eye, we sat round the garden table drinking copious amounts of tea and eating a huge slice of cake, for medicinal purposes only. Sporting an eye that was getting blacker by the minute, I left with my trusty pressure hose, and money in my pocket for my fundraising pot. You will hear about these two later on, yes Ted I have a long memory…..

Another job for my money pot was really a challenge in itself, talked into it over several weeks, 'Life Model Rosie', oh my word, NO, NO, NO, not in a month of Sundays. NEVER, NEVER, NEVER! The pay is good, more money for your pot….well, all I can say, what an experience, you can read all about my 'modelling' in my book 'Why Am I Doing This', also being sold for my charity.

So with all this going on I had to get into training, 10,000 steps a day on my step machine for starters, lots of walking, up hills, down hills, walking on the beach, clambering over rocks, up and down steps, walking in the rain, wind and hot sunshine.

One thing which is pretty important, I don't know the coastal path, yes you say, pretty obvious isn't it, it goes round the outside of the island, or does it….. Obtaining a detailed map sectioned into 7 parts, I began my training programme for real, walking a section at a time, making notes along the way, memorising as much as I could.

The weeks were whizzing by, a slight panic was starting to form inside me, what on earth am I doing, well, no gain without pain, hmm, that was voiced over in my mind many times to come in the following weeks.

I realised to do this on my own would be rather foolish, Peter, who was up from Devon visiting his Aunt and Uncle along the lane, volunteered to come along and be my support vehicle. Another issue I had, night walking, definitely not on my own, I am clumsy during daylight hours, I dread to think what could happen in the dead of the night. Hello Ted, he has been volunteered by Carol to help out. We do not discuss his exact role, instructions nearer the time, very near in fact, so he has no chance of running away.

It is now only a week away, I am thinking of all the ways I can back out, hurt foot, bad back, looks like it might rain!!! No, that is not how I do things. A spin round the island with Peter to locate all the pit stops for refreshments, put me in a frenzy. Since when has the Military Road been that long, Culver Down so high, the paths so treacherous with rocks and tree roots. Yikes, I really am a foolish woman.

Having said that as I have told everyone this is what I am going to do I CANNOT BACK OUT. I do have a golden rule though, if I hurt, STOP, one thing I don't want to do is have an ongoing injury for the rest of my life. The thought of not being able to continue my passion for walking, well…

It is now four days before I start my challenge, I check the weather forecast almost on the hour every hour. It looks warm/hot/ sunny, gosh, how good is that, not a rain cloud to be seen.

Well, I am as fit as I'll ever be, I have stopped most of my training, only doing gentle walks to keep me supple, storing up my energy supplies for the task ahead of me.

I need to concentrate on what to wear and take with me, as it will be chilly during the night, oh my goodness, I stop breathing, gulp for air, chilly during the NIGHT!! Again I am realising the enormity of the task I am about to endure.

With enough clothes for a weeks holiday and more, the van is looking quite full. Peter is sorting the food, so it is only the bits and bobs on the day.

It is Friday night, 17th July, I shower, wash my hair, paint my nails!!, no for goodness sake, this isn't a party, no, but perhaps nice nails might help when things get shall I say a bit difficult, stressed!! Looking at nicely manicured nails might remind me that I 'was' caring about how I looked. Checking that I have everything ready to put on later, (this reminds me of school days, uniform out, shoes polished, satchel packed with COMPLETED homework, well maybe). Right switch off now for five hours, climb into bed and sleep……... Why oh why does my brain start to work on overdrive, have I got this, have I got that. Good gracious, I have been going over everything for weeks.

Catching a bit of sleep my TWO alarms sound off, no that can't possibly be, it's still dark. Realising what I am about to undertake, I burst into tears, oh no, why, why, why, hmm, for my charity that's why.

Kettle on, I dive into the bathroom, ablutions done, a mug of tea. Ah that's better, porridge, yes a lining for my stomach as my Mother used to say. A ping from the microwave it's done, fruit, yogurt, yum, yum…..but alas, three spoonfuls and I'm done, sorry Mum, I really cannot eat porridge at 3 o'clock in the morning. Another mug of tea, yes, lovely.

With leggings, tea shirt and a hoodie on (for extra security I have my name Rosie on the front) as if I would forget my name or get lost!! Right the all important FEET. I smother my feet in vaseline then put on a fine pair of cotton socks, over the top of these my thicker walking socks. I stare at my trusty boots, almost unrecognisable, yes, I have CLEANED THEM FOR THE OCCASION. My hands are shaking as I tie up the laces, I wiggle my toes telling them that I shall take them out of hiding once we have completed 67 miles, oh my word.

With a wistful glance at my bed knowing I won't be in it tonight brings tears and panic, talking to myself very severely I do an about turn, rucksack on my back, pick up my house keys and I'm off. No hang on a minute TORCH it's still dark, I will certainly need it tonight, with that thought, again tears prick my eyes. MOBILE PHONE ROSIE!!! for goodness sake and the charging lead!!!

GURNARD TO YARMOUTH

Stepping outside the air is so fresh I take a deep breath and fill my lungs, instantly feeling so much better, the sky is clear, bright stars are twinkling still, but I can see the sky is starting to lighten from the east.

I walk down the lane and give the 'limo' my support vehicle a pat, saying 'right see you in Yarmouth at 9 o'clock for breakfast'. I glance across the water towards Southampton just at the right moment to see a cruise ship, my what a sight, it looks like a floating candelabra, entering Southampton waters.

Taking a left onto the coastal path, over the first of many stiles, now my journey begins. More deep breathing, with a spring in my step and feeling pretty relaxed I hear something, there it is again, only louder, I nearly jumped out of my skin. Good grief what is it, I start shaking, turning round I see a light on, oh my goodness me, it is Peter's uncle wishing me good luck from the bathroom window. I immediately start laughing, thank him and walk on.

This part of the walk is quite tricky especially as it's still dark, shining my torch I have tree roots, rocks and pathways where they USED to be. So easy to twist my ankle, so I am repeating my golden rule, if I hurt, STOP WALKING, over and over again. I head towards Thorness Bay the sky is getting lighter, the beach looks surreal in the half light with no human on it, only the wildlife enjoying their peace before the bucket and spade brigade arrive. Turning into the camp site I feel

like an intruder, not a sound from anywhere. I have fingers crossed that I don't disturb any dogs and wake up the whole of the camp site. Once through I cross the road to the farm, the path opens out to several fields, some ponies come over to say 'hello', a pat on the nose, theirs not mine, I wish them a good day, and I'm off. Once through the fields it's over a stile, turning right, now it is road walking for several miles. It is getting quite light, gosh the air is so fresh, I just want to drink it in.

Through Porchfield and along the lane I experience the first of many delights, the sun at this point is sending rays of sunshine through the canopy of leafy trees, turning everything golden. Looking up to the sky, tufts of clouds are pink, golden and white. I just stop in awe of what I am seeing, we miss so much when we are asleep in our beds. Moving on, a barn owl flutters past, who jumps the most, him or me. Rabbits, voles, even a rat scampers across my path, suddenly in this quiet lane a hive of activity.

I really do have a spring in my step, swinging my arms to loosen my shoulder and neck muscles. Continuing on to Clamerkin Bridge and turning right to Newtown, eventually passing the National Trust building called 'Noah's Ark' and the Town Hall on my left. This is an easy walk on the flat, past Corf Farm and along to the mill at Shalfleet. The sky is now clear blue with brilliant sunshine, how good is that.

My peace and tranquility is soon gone, walking past the mill my hip is starting to ache, this is an old problem that rears its ugly head every now and again.

A 17th century town hall with no town.
Newtown was once the capital of the Isle of Wight.

No, surely not now, all those months of training and walking, of preparation, not a twinge, it cannot happen now. Turning right past the New Inn on the road towards Yarmouth, I take a seat at the bus stop, no, no readers, I'm not going to hop on a bus; a glug of water and a KitKat, this moment of crisis needs a chocolate fix. While pondering, a bell goes off in my head, simple, problem solved, I think, I am walking toooo fast, in all my weeks of training I never gave it a thought to pace myself. Now refreshed I set off again at a slower pace, with much relief it's working. Thank goodness as I still have about 60 miles to go.

I turn off the main road to my right, over a stile and walk several fields. On approaching a small bridge I sit to retie my boot lace, I stop and listen, nothing, how often do we hear nothing, bliss, quite an experience.

Walking on now I am saying 'good morning ' to some early walkers and joggers, following directions through Hamstead Quay, again how beautiful everything looks, chocolate box picture, a tree lined lane with the quay at the end. Just before the quay I turn left over a stile and negotiate several fields.

Wooden bridge at Hamstead where I listened to silence.

Inquisitive sheep walk up to me, birds singing and a tractor working the fields in the distance, this certainly puts me on a high. I'm only on the first leg of 7, already I am experiencing how beautiful the island is and how much it has to offer. Following the path I reach the shoreline, the water looks very clear and inviting, a paddle perhaps!! NO, I am a woman on a mission with a lot to do.

Carrying on, I pass a memorial stone on the left and continue along the track, I follow the directions through farm land and wooded areas, another shingle beach, until eventually I emerge onto the

Yarmouth road again. Reality hits me, a real road with cars on. A short walk along, then I drop down onto the wall that leads into Yarmouth town. It is 8.45am, perfect for time with my first loo stop coming up on my left. Walking through the centre I am starving, having just walked past a bakery, it took all my will power not to go in, bit useless having those thoughts though, as I don't have any money on me. Rounding the corner I approach the main car park and there's my breakfast stop, hmm, Peter as well.

The day is warming up so I change into my shorts and tee shirt. Woe is me, mega problem, my beloved boots don't feel very comfortable, great cucumbers, what do I do, they are a part of me, have been for years!!! Think, think, diving in the back of the van a decision has to be made. I yank out my trainers…..well thats what they were originally, great cucumbers again, they are my emergency footwear, a 'just in case'….. oh well, one's feet must be comfortable. Saying goodbye to my boots I chuck them in the back of the van, put on my replacement footwear and hope they last to take me round. Looking down they are disgusting, but hey ho, this isn't a fashion show.

YARMOUTH TO FRESHWATER

Having consumed a large bacon roll, replenished my water and KitKat supplies, I am refreshed and ready for part 2 of 7 sections. I am very buoyant with food in my tum, having made arrangements to see Peter at the next 'pit stop' Alum Bay. I set off across the bridge and turn right at the bend of the road, then a left along the sea wall. I continue along reaching Victoria Country Park and walk up into the woods, feeling warm now I am glad of some shady areas. Following directions I walk through to Brambles Chine Holiday Camp, what a beautiful place to have holiday chalets, such wonderful views. Concentrate Rosie, the dreaded hip twinges again….I must pull my pace back, it's so strange I am so unaware of speeding up.

A bit of road walking then I drop down to Colwell Bay, some flat walking where I don't have to think, save my mental energy for Headon Warren. (This is an understatement, on my practice walk I went hopelessly wrong,

WHAT! impossible Rosie, keep the sea on your right…. easy. Well they were my thoughts until I found myself going through so much foliage and so so tall, higher than me, in fact I really thought I was in that film *Honey I Shrank The Kids*).

Now approaching the lifeboat station, I take a few deep breaths and negotiate the steps up towards Widdick Chine. This part is quite difficult because, once at the top of the steps, the path and road wind round very steeply, giving no time to get my breath back. Turning right off the road I start to walk through Headon Warren, thank goodness the foliage has started to die down, I can now see right across Alum Bay to the needles, another amazing view, a few deep breaths and I'm on top of the world, literally, my goodness me I feel great, one really hopes I continue like this until I reach Gurnard….hmmm.

In the distance I can just see the 'red limo', great, could murder a mug of coffee.

At this stage Peter starts nagging me to drink plenty of water, yeah, yeah, as I replenish my water bottles. A bit of banter, changing my tee shirt for a vest top, I'm all set for the next bit. Really thankful that my feet are very snug in my 'designer' trainers, off I go. Lunch is at Freshwater, so with a lightness of step and full of positive thoughts I make my way through the crowds of holiday makers.

I take the well worn path up to the Needles. This feels strange, usually I am walking in the other direction down towards Alum Bay, having near completion of our hospice walk across the island, all I'm doing then is following the crowd, oblivious to the scenery, as I am near to exhaustion. Crikey that was only 26 miles, this is 67, Rosie, Rosie, Rosie what are you doing……

 Once I reach the Needles and turn I mentally get a buzz, I am now walking towards the most southerly part of the island, really feel I am achieving. It is a beautiful part of the island with far reaching views, miles of sea to the right, with gentle waves lapping onto the beach, they seem to be happy like me on such a beautiful morning. On my left rolling countryside, people walking, excited

dogs running round, farmers working their fields. Beyond is the Solent, so many sailing boats with their white and brightly coloured sails, zig zagging their way up and down with the flow of the water. In the far distance the mainland and the New Forest. The weather is perfect with a slight breeze keeping me cool. At Alum Bay I discarded my rucksack for a bum bag giving me complete freedom of movement with my arms.

View form Headon Warren looking over to Alum Bay and the Needles.

A wonderful walk down Tennyson, letting my mind and body relax, some deep breathing that I learnt from my yoga classes many years ago, hopefully storing some mental and physical energy.

At the bottom of Tennyson Down I can just see Freshwater loos, a welcome sight. I do have to speed up a tad as I am beginning to feel desperate. Going straight in, thank goodness no queue, never did I think a loo seat could feel like a comfy armchair. Whilst sitting I take off my shorts and knickers, discard the latter on the floor and rummage in my bag for a fresh pair. Taking out my water bottle

I realise I didn't put the top on properly, no, NO!!! WET KNICKERS. What a twit, I now have a decision to make 'wet' knickers or worn ones discarded on a public loo floor. Well, if I say I know what a baby feels like wearing a wet nappy you can decide what pair I chose.

Walking to the sea front I recognise a person sitting on a seat, TED, wow, how good is that. He and Carol are parked further up in the car park and have bought a picnic and moral support. Peter is at the ready with a mug of tea and ham rolls. Lots of chatting and laughter, until a firm voice very calmly reminds me, get going Rosie!! How right he was as I am beginning to stiffen, standing up and adjusting my still damp apparel, with hugs and kisses wishing me luck, I turn and walk away. Glancing over my shoulder I casually mention 'SEE YOU TONIGHT TED', I don't wait for a reply, (he still thinks he is meeting me in Cowes TOMORROW and walking me to Gurnard!!), as arranged Carol will be waiting for my phone call later on. Again in good spirits I walk with a purpose looking forward to walking the Military Road as it is so beautiful.

'Don't like that photo Ted'

FRESHWATER TO VENTNOR

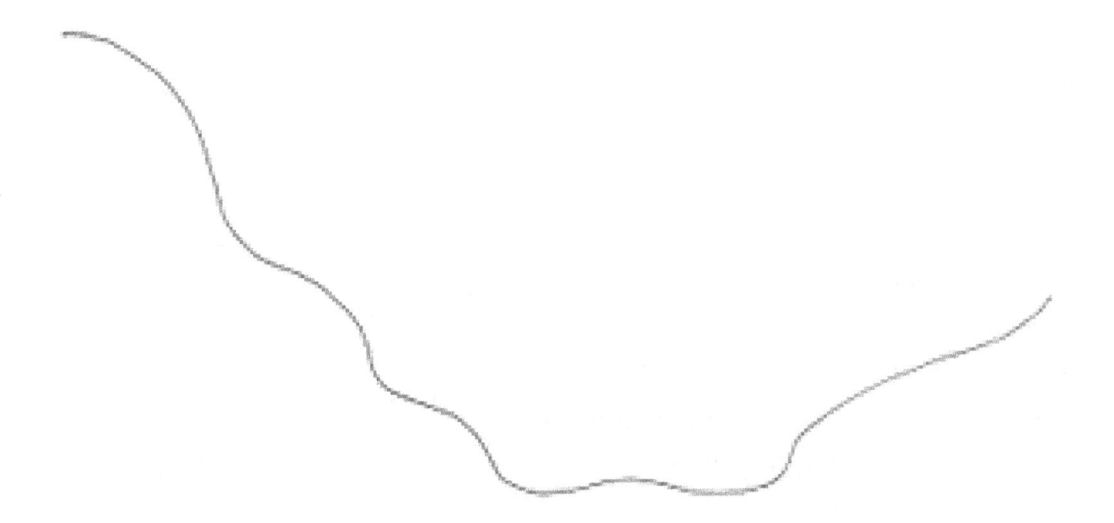

Slow down for goodness sake, I am now getting a tad cross with myself, it is so difficult getting the pace right. I suppose in all my practice walks and learning the route I never did more than 20 miles, so it never came into the equation. The sea breeze is lovely keeping me cool but after about an hour it turned into a cross wind making my walking a little difficult. Having to adjust I can feel my legs aching and my shoulders, what do I do now. I am exposed to an onshore wind for quite a few miles. This is distressing me, as I thought this would be an easy part of the route. I need an emergency plan, think, think,...... I know if I walk along the road the hedging will act as a windbreak, it isn't all along the roadside but what there is will at least give me a bit shielding from the wind. And so I made my way across the field and started road walking, yes before you ask, against the traffic.

This lasted for about 10 minutes, I now had another decision to make, battle the wind or risk being FLAT PACKED. Come on drivers give me a break, be kind…...and so I made my way across the field to be once again on the coastal path. All those extra strides and time wasted crossing the field I could of done without. It was at this point a few swear words crept in, no readers I will leave you to your imagination as to the ones I chose. Peter must have sensed my mood, so extra 'pit stops' along the Military Road were arranged, if only for me to vent my anger about selfish drivers!!!

Plodding (yes it was plodding at this stage) I eventually made my way up to the viewing point, passing the entrance to Blackgang Chine, an unscheduled pit stop, one of many to come, a bit of chatter to lighten my mood, I set off again.

I am disappointed with my walk from Freshwater to Blackgang, I was certain it would be plain sailing with the pretty chines and quaint clusters of homes and farms, a really beautiful part of the island. I'm having to work on myself mentally and physically, as the hardest part of the walk is yet to come.

Leaving the viewing point, I'm on a well defined part of the path so, once again, I can let my mind rest. Concern is drifting in, I am running late so I have said to Peter it will probably be about 8 o'clock when I reach Ventnor, much, much too late by my calculations, but I can do nothing about it.

Walking along the Undercliff I have a glorious view of St Catherine's Lighthouse in the late afternoon sun, this relaxes me, again I pull back my pace and enjoy. Realising at this point that I started the day with fresh morning sunshine, with beautiful lights streaming over fields and filtering through leafy trees, finishing with deep golden rays spreading across the fields and cliffs, a perfect day of wall to wall sunshine.

Automated in 1997, with keepers leaving on 30th July

A loo stop is needed, just find the right bush with no thorns and stinging nettles. I am aware of changing direction, now heading east, have I really walked this far. I am weary but no aches or pains, or the dreaded blisters, a big slug of water, I can now enjoy a wonderful sunset while I drop down stone steps to the Seven Sisters Road at St Lawrence. I must concentrate on my directions here, getting myself back onto the coastal path at Woody Bay. Once on this path I am fine for a few miles as I have walked this part of the path many times.

Walking past Orchard House my text goes, I haven't encouraged people to contact me as I didn't want to keep stopping, first to find my phone, then my glasses. Also I would be out of time with my pacing, this is so energy consuming, really important for me to have ' energy in storage' for tonight and tomorrow morning, very precious for me to have a big reserve in the tank. It is Julie from our Island Hospice, she is a day patient who I befriended, she lives near the chain ferry and wants to know what time I shall be at the ferry TOMORROW!!! Well how long is a piece of string? We decide that as long as it isn't before 7 o'clock I will walk round the corner from the chain ferry to

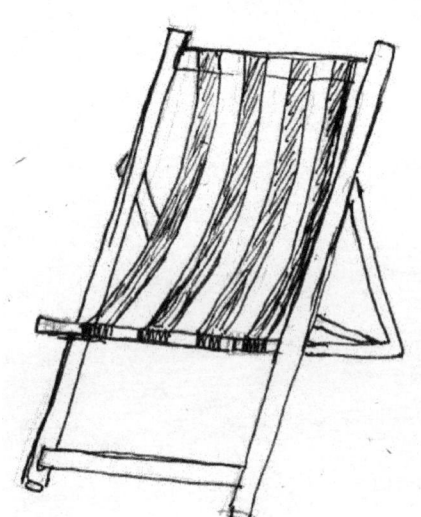

see them as they want to give me a hug and moral support, methinks by then I shall definitely need it.

I am now dropping down to Steep Hill Cove, magical, the sun is just about setting, warmth in abundance still, families enjoying the beach, children in the water. This place always reminds me of my childhood, it is so much in the 50s/60s style. Unspoilt, very quiet, blue and white striped deck chairs, no slot machines, music etc, bliss. I'm very tempted to sit on a rock and ponder ....no Rosie, Ventnor calls.

Approaching Ventnor it is easy to see the limo in the now almost empty car park. I am about an hour later than I wanted to be, you will understand the full meaning of this shortly.

Standing with my always needed mug of tea, chitchat about the next part of my walk, I assure Peter that although the light is fading everything will be FINE. I put on my warmer clothing, a dubious look at my trainers, yes they are holding up, I then set off for Shanklin, our next 'pit stop'. Yes, yes Peter the next bit to Bonchurch and beyond is pretty 'cool', easy walking. Sounding more positive than I really was, I set off.

No slot machines or music here.

VENTNOR TO YAVERLAND

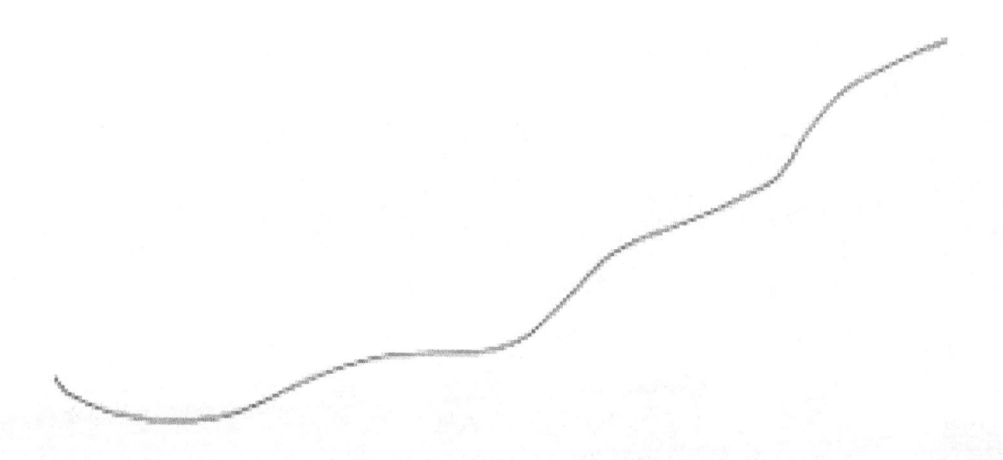

The walk to Bonchurch is flat and ideal to get me loosened up so I do a power walk, lengthening my stride, stretching my hip muscles. Arriving at the bottom of some very steep steps I am rooted to the spot. I am very much aware of how dark it is, looking up, the top has disappeared in the last of the light. Oh my goodness, I cannot do this, I DON'T DO DARK!! especially on my own. This is why I was concerned about being behind schedule. Now comes my yoga breathing to calm me down, scrambling in my bag for my torch, JUST GET UP THOSE STEPS ROSIE!!

Once at the top I follow the path leaving the houses behind and walk through the copse to Bonchurch Old Church. My mouth is very dry, it is as much as I can do to stay positive. This area is called the 'Landslip', not encouraging is it. Compose yourself Rosie, I'm sorry readers you will find from now to the end of my walk that I talk or shout much to myself!! Right a slug of water, a strip of chewing gum, I'm ready. The terrain is now very difficult, I use my torch for my feet to give them a bit of comfort to know where to put themselves. At the other end of my body, fear and near to tears, I know I have to persevere, no going back. Certainly don't let negative thoughts come into my mind, 'what if I get lost, will anyone remember me, what if a grizzly bear jumps out and eats me up, leaving only my torch on the ground.. Oh come on Rosie, grown woman and all that…..I know, start singing, that's better, I cannot sing, but who cares, no one around, OR IS THERE!!

Stopping to read my directions I just hope I have it right, where is that bloody 'wishing seat'. Alas it is quite a bit further on, methinks it is 'wishful' thinking. A branch flaps in my face and I scream and jump back, I flash my torch to make sure I am on my own. Singing out of the question, I am far too nervous.

So I'm told, sit on it and make a wish and your wish will come true. What if you run up to it, give it a hug and cry with relief.

Why oh why is my mind working against me, I am now taken back to the *Noddy* books that I read as a child and I now read to my great- granddaughters. I'm sure you all remember the 'gollies and goblins' in the woods, oh crikey, will I ever get out of this bloody 'landslip'. Further on I can see a black lump of rock looking vaguely familiar, yes the wishing seat, screams of joy I hug this dirty ole lump of rock and continue on my journey. Feeling a tad better now I talk to myself all the time, negotiating the ongoing difficult terrain.

I plod along until I come out of the wooded area and walk through a garden belonging to a very nice man called George. The coastal path cuts through his land which I think he rather likes because people love to stop and chat. This is what happened on my practice walks, chat, chat, chat, a cuppa and much to my delight while sitting on his veranda, I fed not 1 not 2 but 3 red squirrels, one even sitting on my trainer. My goodness me Mr Squirrel you wouldn't do that now, I can whiff my feet from 5ft 7ins away, yuck, and I still have a long way to go.

It was arranged that I would call in on my walk for a cuppa, hmm, says me, see you about 7 o'clock, well as you know I am well out with my timing, it is now 10 o'clock. So as not to disturb him I start to creep past his patio doors. Half way along, Blackpool Illuminations, brightness everywhere, all his security lights came on, oh my, what do I do, he is sitting in front of the television doing a crossword, instantly he looks up to see this very sorry looking 'thing' at his patio door. I'm very near to tears, he wants me to go in for a cuppa, no, no, no, I cannot possibly, I am terribly late and need to get to Shanklin. He had thought I had abandoned my walk and never expected to see me at this hour.

'Abandoned George, given up, HUH' no way. Sensing my fear of the dark, being very stressed, near to tears, my huge struggle, weary damsel in distress, etc etc, being the perfect gentleman, he donned his coat, walking boots, a very large torch that had the power to light up the whole of the island and more, lead me safely to the lane, where I would drop down into Shanklin. Bless you George you're a star.

Thank heavens, street lights, houses with lights on, civilisation. One thing on my mind, loo. Crossing the park area I head straight for the green door, OUCH, that hurt, rubbing my forehead I rattle the catch, oh for goodness sake, LOCKED, doesn't anyone need the loo after 10 o'clock!!!! I try the gents to no avail. Think, think, Rosie, only one option left, sorry people of Shanklin your beautiful begonias had an extra watering tonight, I'm sure they blossomed well for weeks.

Now I need to find the steps that go down to the beach, well, everyone knows this part, so I didn't actually rehearse this bit. With over a hundred steps it must be well lit up, surely…..where are they, walking up and down along the path, now feeling panicky WHERE ARE THE BLOODY STEPS. So much for well lit up, it is as black as the ace of spades. My goodness I'm wasting energy and TIME…HELP!!!!

Walking further along the path a rather posh hotel comes into view, dare I go in, a description of myself in one word TRAMP, a smelly one as well. Right, just got to go for it, the worse thing they can do is throw me out. Tip toeing in on a beautiful carpet I approach the receptionist, she smiled sweetly, asking my question about steps and beach, her reply was that she didn't know, hmm, but she would call the chef. Out came this very jolly guy, 'Yes, yes, you will find them a little way up the path'. With that he came out of the front door with me, pointing a finger in the right direction. Warning me to be careful as they are very uneven and no lights to guide me, by now I really don't care, I just want to get to the car park and see the limo. Thanking him I start off once again.

With my torch on I proceed slowly down, holding onto the rail to help with my balance as my legs are feeling a tad wobbly. Wow, yes, uneven is the word, thank goodness it's not raining and I add 'slippery' to my description. At last down on the beach, although pitch dark here, I can see the lights of Shanklin, and…..what a glorious sight….the red limo is parked under a street light.

'You took your time, problems Rosie?' inquired Peter.

'No, bit uneventful really, just make the tea. PLEASE!! came my reply in a nonchalant voice

At this moment Carol and Ted arrived, I really need them at Yaverland, so as politely as I could I ask them to meet me there, oh and could you buy some more water please. Not sure how they replied…..

The walk to Yaverland is on concrete and flat so I decide to do another power walk to stretch and loosen up my hips and legs again. My mobile phone needs charging so I hand it over to Peter, unless the lights are switched off at a certain time along the esplanade, I have good vision and feel confident that my phone wouldn't be needed. I set off feeling pretty refreshed, my head is in a good place. A group of young lads sitting on the wall shout out cheeky things to me, I smile but don't engage in conversation with them, walking on I just hope upon hope they don't follow me. What a time NOT to have my phone!!!! a quick look back, they have forgotten me, I can relax again.

YAVALAND TO SEAVIEW

Arriving at Yaverland it is now midnight, Carol and Ted have joined us, bacon and egg rolls, lots of tea and coffee, gosh, I am such a pig, eating huge amounts, I shall be a round ball by the time I finish. I am assured that I am using up vast amounts of calories and need to eat.

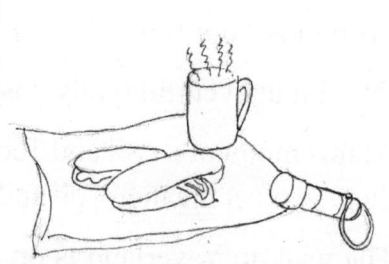

Right banter over, serious discussion,

'Which way Rosie?' asks an apprehensive Ted.

'Well, see that black mound over yonder Ted', came an almost flippant reply from me.

'Er, yes Rosie' replied Ted in a very, very apprehensive voice. I think Ted is shaking now.

'Well' says I again ' we are going to climb over it', glancing at Ted had we been standing under a street lamp his face I'm sure would have been very white, his body language told me he was poised to RUN in the opposite direction.

Ignoring this thought I made sure we had plenty of water, KitKats, torches, lights on our hats like miners, we are ready. Carol is to go back home and wait for a phone call from Peter to say 'pick Ted up'.

So with cheerful goodbyes, see you at Bembridge Lifeboat Station, we start to stride out.

'Rosie, do you know the way', asks a tentative Ted

'Yeah, yeah, yeah, says I with confidence, 'just follow the barbed wire fencing'. Well that was ok until we realised the path was only 18 inches wide, a sheer drop down the cliff on our right, hmm, I think I have gone wrong.

'Ted I think we need to be the other side of the fence', says I trying to keep the concern out of my voice.

Being sensible and intelligent it was decided we 'hop' over onto the other side, simple, no, it's a new fence with no 'give' in it. To anyone who has experienced this, barbed wire is evil. I know, I know, it's supposed to be. A moments silence then my 'gallant' friend suggested he put his rucksack on top of the wire forming a saddle, wow, how good is that. I really cannot remember how he achieved his task, but words like 'tackle, risk, never be the same again, were the words he used. Moving on we had the steep climb up Culver Down to the monument, believe it or not we were walking across and up, much too far over to 'find' this lump of stone. Why, oh why, don't we have a moon tonight, it is as black as the ace of spades. Feeling panicky now a voice behind me

'Is it very big' asks Ted in a squeaky voice.

'Is it very big Rosie', squeaked Ted, pretty fearful of my reply.

W-e-l-l, shall I just say my language wasn't that of a 'lady'. A while later, much to our relief, we could just make out the monument in the night sky, cheers and giggles released all the nervous tension, now we are getting somewhere. Giving the monument a hug 'thank you Earl of Yarborough for putting this lump of stone here'.

Walking down a field which seems to be twice as long, twice as wide in the dark, we now have a chalky path that drops down steeply to White Cliff bay, tension again as the chalky stones are loose and our footing is very slippy.

Making our way through to Bembridge was quite complicated, referring to our directions and map frequently, especially when we approached a large sign COASTAL PATH CLOSED TO EROSION, with a red arrow pointing to the left,……. that was it, find your own way. HUH!

Weaving our way inland, through an estate of mainly bungalows, passing the well-known Crab & Lobster Pub we eventually found ourselves at the lifeboat station car park and that red limo. Oh what joy!!

It is now 2 o, clock, way off my timing but now it is just a case of getting back to Gurnard, whew, did I really say that.….A quick few words and we are off, the cooler air is playing havoc with my calf muscles must keep on the move. It is decided we have a picnic in a sheltered spot at Bembridge harbour.

Slight hiccup here, walking towards the beach I hadn't built into the equation TIDES, NO, NO, NO, where has all this water come from. On my practice walk it was BEACH! Oh come on Rosie, the water moves in and out, everyone knows that. Now I am seriously wondering how I have managed

to get this far in my life.…...WET SUITS ANYONE (this is another title to one of my stories in WHY AM I DOING THIS). With the limo still in view we decide to follow Peter through roads with more bungalows. His headlights pick out 4 foxes on our way.

'Don't make eye contact Ted, you would make a delicious night time snack, but me, well, methinks I smell a tad not too wholesome even for a fox. (little did I know what another 9 hours of walking would do to my personal hygiene). Peter drives off to the harbour as we know the way, he gets the chairs out, kettle on for our 'picnic'. Some serious discussion is needed, bit of laughter and banter again to help my mental state and we are ready for the off.

A short walk to the Duver at St Helen's proves mentally very, very difficult as I am going through a bad patch, really wanting to call it a day….NO, I don't hurt, so keep going. It is 3 o'clock I have been going for 23 hours, oh my word….I picture my empty bed, no don't do that.

Walking past the houseboats I ask Ted to chat, sorry for the life of me I cannot remember a word of our conversation, but I'm sure it helped. We have now walked through to the mill at St Helens, looking for the sign OLD DAM WALL, once found, standing in front of this crumbling uneven causeway Ted exclaims in horror,

Doesn't look very dangerous in the daylight but in the black of the night having walked for 23 hours and legs that are a little bit wobbly

'NO ROSIE IT IS DANGEROUS we can't see properly, one slip……...'

'Look on the bright side, we have torches, it's not windy or raining, so many pluses Ted, and the limo will be at the beach with a cuppa at the ready. Follow me Ted, slow but sure, you will be safe'. I hope I have quelled his nerves.

So, very, very gingerly with my legs that won't seem to do as I tell them, we made our way across to safety. I think Ted held his breath all the way, he looks a bit peculiar, I kid myself that it's just the light from my torch.

On the beach at the Duver I find the loos open, HURRAH, oh to sit down, what luxury. With a mug of tea at the ready and a banana, I walk away from the lads, suddenly I am feeling antisocial, miserable, tearful, sorry for myself, thinking of my comfy bed again, until……. a booming voice hits my ears,

'COME ON ROSIE NO TIME TO PONDER, GET ON WITH IT', shouts Peter.

'OKAY' I shout back, 'BLEEP, BLEEP, BLEEP'. Oh my goodness I am so stiff, do get a grip Rosie.

We cross the road at the Old Church Lodge, approaching a stile, this is where I really get into serious difficulties.

Ted being the perfect gentleman, AGAIN, he lets me hop up first, hop being the operative word, lots of creaks and groans, not the stile I hasten to add, ME!! Making sure I am balanced safely I throw my right leg over, then as I thought, the usual flick with my left leg, only to find it won't move…..

'Oh my word Ted, I can't get my 'leg over' with this we look at each other and burst into laughter. I am straddling the stile, not being able to go this way, that way, any which way, heavens what a predicament to be in at 4 o'clock in the morning. Composure found somehow Ted grabs my leg with both hands and throws it over, oh how elegant, again helpless laughter erupts. Thankfully he leaps over the stile, well sort of and asks for directions.

'Right, cross the field, over a stile, through an area of scrub land, diagonally across another field, find a metal gate, leaning on it's side, go through, onto a lane and turn right'. I cannot print his reply but was politely told to take the lead. Again lots of laughter relieving the tension.

We continue towards the Priory Hotel and take a left at the white gates, down a bridleway with a field on the left. It is still very dark so progress is slow but sure. Once we come out of the wooded area I can see the sky is starting to lighten, oh joy, upon joy, this really gives me a buzz.

Following the road round we drop down to the esplanade at Seagrove Bay. It is difficult for me to focus on the beautiful colours of the sky, which is getting lighter by the minute, as my eyes are so sore and puffy they feel and look like slits on my face.

'Excuse me did you speak to me Ted', bringing me back to reality again.

'Yes Rosie, I'm all in, I cannot possibly walk any further'. Poor man he has done amazingly. I haven't given him a thought how he is feeling, how selfish is that. Without him I couldn't have done it, even just from the safety angle. To walk in the night on my own, would have been absolute stupidity.

He takes a good look at me

'Rosie, you look dreadful, why don't you call it a day, you've done so well, we are all proud of you.......

'Well Ted, it's like this NO, bleep, NO, bleep, NO, bleep. Thank you for saying and your concern. My pact with myself is 'IF I HURT, STOP', well I don't actually hurt, (but I am questioning my mental state though). 'No I will be fine'.

'We must get hold of Carol', hmm, 5 o'clock in the morning, hmm again, well we are good friends.......so far!

SEAVIEW TO RYDE

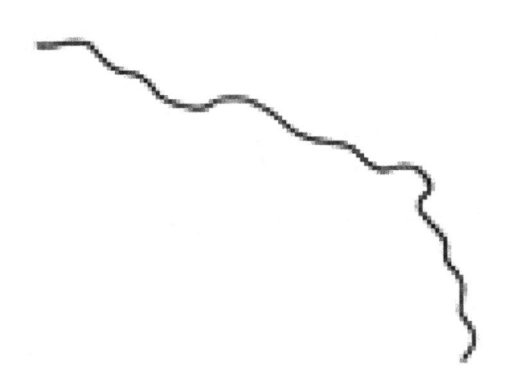

We cannot get hold of Carol so Peter suggests he takes Ted home as long as I can reassure him that I will be ok. YES, YES, of course I will be, easy walk along Ryde Esplanade, no one around, beautiful summer morning, what could possibly go wrong.

'Come on off you go', getting impatient I walk off, full of determination, I think not. Watching the limo pull away, getting smaller in the distance I feel so desolate…... all alone in the world is me…... I am ready to curl up…... and die……. in a smelly ball……

No Rosie that's not healthy thinking, look a seat along the wall, a glug of water and yes another KitKat, just the job. While munching and talking to myself I look up to see this enormous red ball sitting on the horizon, wow, how amazing is that, but…..for a split second I didn't know whether it was sunrise or sunset. Do I laugh, cry, be happy, sad. Everything feels floaty, surreal, Hell's bells, how worrying is that, am I going to make it YES!! shaking my head which made it hurt and me dizzy, I stood up, stretched, deep breaths, SUNRISE you nincompoop, look it's going up OFF the water, not DOWN below.

So problem solved, feeling 'refreshed' I started to make my way to the other side of Ryde. This was very pleasant, now saying 'good morning' to early joggers and dog walkers.

Continuing in a world of my own, I was suddenly jolted back into life, by this screech of brakes from a car, approaching from behind, now pulling in level with me, grinding to an emergency stop, bewildered, I turned my head, window wound down, it's Carol.

'Where are they for goodness sake' shouted Carol

'Oh' came my reply, 'Peter has taken Ted back home'

'Oh for BLEEP, BLEEP sake, they couldn't organise a piss up in a brewery!!

With that, window up, foot hard on the 'gas' as they say, a racing start, off she roared.

Only to stop a few yards away, slam the car in reverse, window down

'Oh, how are you Rosie'

'Fine Carol' and off she roared again leaving me speechless on the pavement.

Poor Carol dragged out of bed, coming all the way from Gurnard, no Ted to be seen anywhere.

Believe it or not that episode kept me laughing until I reached the other end of Ryde.

Arriving at the car park I sat on the wall and waited for Peter, now I really am in a mess, my limbs are stiff, I smell sweaty, eyes are like puff balls and I want to howl my eyes out. I look at my rucksack and see it as a comfy pillow, this hard stone wall feels like a feather mattress. No, no for goodness sake DON'T LIE DOWN, sit up, think of something else. Hmm, I start counting the windows on the building opposite, I watch a woman come out of her flat and get into her car.

Oh for goodness sake Peter HURRY UP, WHAT'S TAKING SO LONG!!!

He must have heard my near hysterical screams for down the hill comes the red limo. He parks, gets out of the van and immediately says

'My God you look like a haggard old bag' Well, the words were hardly out of his mouth when I literally flew at him, a verbal attack, stamping my feet like a three year old, fists in the air,

'Don't talk to me like that you bleep, bleep, bleep, yes and another bleep. With tears streaming down my face another few seconds I reckon I would of punched him, well, try, he was after all 6ft 2inches and 19 stone. Hmm.

'Soft' wall at Ryde….I desperately need my bed

Very calmly I was told that was the response he wanted, would I like to sit down, drink my tea, eat my ham roll, take in a few deep breaths to prepare myself for the next section of the walk.

Laughing now, crisis over for a while, everything looked brighter.

RYDE TO GURNARD

This is the last leg of my walk, only 11 miles to go but it might just as well have been 11,000,000,000,000. I'm really having to concentrate on my directions as I've only walked this part once, in some ways that is good, taking my mind off how I am feeling. The route is interesting, lots of twists and turns, past the golf course, church, Abbey Ruins and Quarr Abbey itself, but at the same time my brain doesn't want to function. To help myself, I go through the relaxation I was taught years ago when I went to yoga. This is working very well on my body, relaxing my limbs, releasing most of the tension, especially across the shoulders. The day is brightening up so I put on my sunglasses, my eyes are so sore I cannot cope with any brightness.

At last I am not far from the Wightlink Ferry at Fishbourne, I have a plan of action. I have my wash bag and a change of clothes in the limo, I so want to clean my teeth. It is still early so I am sure the place will be deserted.

I am livid, how wrong can I be, the 'Ladies' which is a smart new block, is heaving with a coach load of …..hmmm…. ladies of a certain age. All chatting and laughing, discussing Mrs so-and-so, and 'what about Ethel's new hat'!! Oh goodness me I want to kick, scream and shout, go away everyone, I booked this place for me, all I want is 10 minutes to freshen up, as they say, or in my case 'scrub up'. Finding just about enough room to squeeze through and clean my teeth, lady next to me, reapplying her lipstick, gives me a disgusting look, not sure if thats from my 'perfume' or me spitting in the basin. So wrong of me but I cannot find the energy to explain what I am doing and

QUARR ABBEY

Looking pretty impressive in the fresh blue of the morning sky.

the reason for my, shall I say, unwholesome state. I felt they all moved away from me as I seemed to have a bit more room. I dive into the loo and change my 'under garments'. Lashings of deodorant on to cover the pong, I'm ready, scoop up my discarded clothes into a carrier bag and escape as quickly as possible, much to their relief.

'Feel better' came a chirpy question from Peter.

"NO' end of conversation, I throw my bag in the back of the van, slam the sliding door and march off. A few seconds later I think I can hear some shouting, turning round Peter is franticly waving his arms.

'WHATS THE MATTER' I'm really annoyed now having to turn round and interrupt my stride.

'YOU ARE WALKING IN THE MIDDLE OF THE ROAD; bellows Peter.

'Oh thanks' came my ungrateful reply. Huh, keep ordering me about……

I turn right off the road by the letter box and proceed through woodland, passing a few houses. My concentration is so bad at times I haven't a clue where I am.

At last I come to the main road that takes me to Wootton Bridge, arrangements have been made to meet Peter at the Sloop Inn. I have to cross the road as there is no path on this side, well that's no problem, or is it! Something we do all the time 'crossing the road', but I am very hesitant, I make sure I am crossing where there is an island in the middle, but even then I don't want to cross. I can only describe my feelings by saying I have become detached, my head and mind from my body, my limbs from my central trunk. Think Rosie, concentrate, after a few moments I make a dash to the island, brill, now I almost run to the pavement, relieved that I have made it.

Approaching the pub I can see Peter, for goodness sake he is shouting at me AGAIN! Well I'm going to have words with him, this is totally out of order, he is taking advantage of my poorly state

'WHY ARE YOU SHOUTING AT ME' I bellow across the road.

'YOU ARE LOOKING BUT NOT SEEING, DO YOU WANT TO BE FLAT PACKED?, WAIT FOR ME TO COME AND SEE YOU ACROSS'.He bellowed back.

'HUH' is all I could say, again!

We have a chat, I am really crying now, I cannot do anymore, a hug, two more minutes of tears and I am told to GO! With that Peter points me in the direction I am to walk, then he gets in the limo, 'Thanks' came my retort and I stomp off.

Quite a bit of pavement walking, feeling quieter now I amuse myself by looking at people's gardens, giving them a score out of 10 for attractiveness. This engages my brain for a while but also brings sadness, very, very few people have what I call a traditional garden with flowers and grass. I understand why they have to be car parks I would probably do the same, but……

Absorbing nothing in my brain I do ask people directions at every junction. I am approaching the second lot of lockup garages, that is good, Church Road into Palmers Road, and yes, there is the rock I remember on my practice walk outside Palmer's Farm. I must sit for a glug of water. I am talking to myself quite a lot now, is it madness or comfort, lets go for comfort, a bit of stretching and I'm ready.

Not far to go now, down the dip, over the bridge at Palmer's Brook, then climb up the other side.

SUDDENLY a huge wave of tiredness comes over me, I feel rooted to the spot, my body won't move, good grief what is happening to me, a stroke…..am I going to die, have I over stretched myself…..GET A GRIP….DEEP BREATHS…..DEEP BREATHS…..FILL MY LUNGS….CALM DOWN, with that I do an enormous stretch, arms in the air, fold myself over to touch my toes and relax my body. I do this a few times, gradually I am returning to normal, I can move. Shaking my legs and arms, rolling my head round, I breath in as much as I can, I am ready to tackle that monster of an incline.

On reaching the Alverstone Road there is Peter, limo parked halfway between me and the post box at the end of the road. He is walking towards me,

'Thought you might need some extra encouragement' with that he holds my hand and walks as far as the van, he then gets in, opens the window, 'see you at the post box', and drives off.

Not a word passes my lips I haven't the energy to speak, I am truly grateful for his support, keeping the promise of a cuppa in my mind gets me to the top of the road.

Chair at the ready I slump down and enjoy my mug of tea and yet another KitKat, I must say for a long while after my walk, KitKats were certainly a no, no.

Even this rock looks like a soft cushion.

Looking at Peter I don't think either of us is going to make it to Gurnard. Having to hang around for me is probably just as hard or worse than doing the actual walk. I never gave him a thought how he must be feeling, how selfish is that. Bless the man.

Arranging to meet him at the chain ferry we both set off. Walking on the main road I kid myself it will be easier as it's downhill, BUT, my toes scrunch up in my trainers, oh boy what pain, after 60 odd miles what can I expect. My ankles are stiff, I'm walking as if I have wet myself. Jeepers when will I get to the end of this bloody road. Thank goodness we have sunshine, with my sunglasses on nobody can see my tears running down my face, I can taste the saltiness in my mouth. Come on Rosie, show some anger now, where is that BLOODY CHAIN FERRY.

The old chain ferry, looks very small compared to our big modern one.

At this stage I just cannot pull out any positive thoughts, I just go with the flow, feeling miserable, wretched, weary and all the other negative emotions I can pull out of the bag. Now walking through East Cowes, seeing happy holiday makers enjoying a beautiful day, I round the corner to see the chain ferry approach

'COME ON ROSIE **RUN** OR YOU WILL MISS IT' boomed Peter, turning everyone's heads to see who he was shouting at.

I **CAN'T RUN YOU FOOL, MY FEET WON'T WORK, BLEEP, BLEEP, BLEEP** and so, from tears to anger in a split second, my that's an achievement in itself. Now we have caught everyone's attention, they are watching and listening, either with amusement or disgust, I just don't care.

Whether Peter got them to hold on for me I don't know as this piece of work is Peter's .....

'Apparently', I stormed onto the ferry, shouted at Peter

'WHERE ARE THE BOILED SWEETS'

In a normal voice 'In the back of the van' informed Peter.

Apparently again, I grunted, tugged open the sliding door of the van, giving it such a whack Peter feared it would come off it's runners, foraging through everything to find MY sweets. Stuffing my pockets, not offering any to Peter, I slammed the door shut. Not acknowledging him, I went and sat where the

foot passengers go. I believe this is an accurate account, to this day I do not remember that crossing. Storming off to go round the corner to say hello to Julie and her husband, Peter made the decision to go to Gurnard and pick up his uncle to walk me home…

Meanwhile I arrive at Julie's.

'Come in, come in, sit down have some breakfast' cried an excited Julie. My what a fantastic welcome and boy so tempting, but…...

'NO, NO, I mustn't stop otherwise I will never start again. You would both be extremely brave, to let me in, I look and smell like a tramp'.

With a hug from each of them I turn round and make my direction towards Cowes High Street. Thank goodness not many people around yet, it is only 10 o'clock on Sunday morning.

'Oh, what happened to Saturday'???

My walking is none too straight methinks I had better make out I am looking in the shop windows, otherwise I could easily be mistaken for a drunk. A 'left over from Saturday night'. I vaguely remember walking through Cowes, my head is so swimming with fatigue, I do so desperately want to be home. P-L-E-A-S-E…….

Walking past the cannons a familiar figure was approaching me, Bill, Peter's uncle (man at the bathroom window) that is really, really good. I believe he chatted all the way back to Gurnard, I don't really know. Apparently I looked so ghastly Peter was worried I would collapse, no way was he going to see me fail, not at this late stage of the walk, so reinforcements were at the ready. Peter is moving slowly up the road keeping me in sight 'just in case'.

Cannons at Cowes

On reaching the beach huts at Gurnard, Bill asks me which way I want to go, the tide is 'out' so do I want to go along the beach and do a bit of rock climbing, or up and over Solent View Road.

Oh my word I was so rude, '**I don't bleep, bleep, know. For goodness sake don't ask me**'.

A calm reply from Bill, 'right we will go along the beach'.

Jeepers I felt every rock, pebble, grain of sand. I think by this time the soles of my trainers were wafer thin. Every stone I walked on, pain shot up my body straight into my head, I don't care about people seeing me cry, or hear me swear, I WANT TO GO HOME!

Picking our way round and over the rocks the finish is in sight.

Through blurred eyes I can see the sea wall, I climb up and walk along. So I'm told afterwards, everyone held their breath, apparently I was swaying with every stride, huh, I don't believe them, do you!!

My word I am back at Dora and Bills place, congratulations all round, I slump into an armchair totally exhausted.

'Cup of tea Rosie', asks Dora.

'Yes please, make it in a bucket, I am so parched.

Someone comments that I have aged 20 years…..what the heck, do I care,

I have just walked round the Isle of Wight in One Hit, taking 31 hours nonstop.

After several mugs of tea and chatter, I am helped out of the arm chair and make a move to get myself up the road to my chalet, Carol comes with me just in case…..in case of what…..

'YOU FALL AND HURT YOURSELF'!!

Very sensible Carol.

At last I am unlocking the door, I slump on a chair in my conservatory to remove my trainers.

This is how my mind was working... undoing my laces, oh my goodness, what if my feet have become detached from my ankles, what if they are all bloody and raw, stuck to my socks, hmm, well, stop the 'what ifs' and take off those disgusting trainers. Flipping heck, surely that smell is not coming from MY feet, I look around, only Carol here, don't even go there Rosie, no way can she be responsible, so I guess it must be me. Trainers are thrown outside, methinks a decent cremation when someone has a bonfire. Thank you very much for getting me round the island.

I peel off both pairs of socks and cannot believe what I am seeing, how brilliant is that, only 2 tiny pink places on the side of both heals, nothing to give me pain. Not a drop of blood, no blisters, no raw bits. Had they not smelt so awful I would have kissed them 'WELL DONE FEET I AM VERY PROUD OF YOU'.

Carol stays while I have a shower, absolute bliss, after which I am more than ready to fall into bed. I set the alarm for 6 o'clock that gives me 6 hours sleep, hopefully then after a meal I can zonk out for a normal night's sleep.

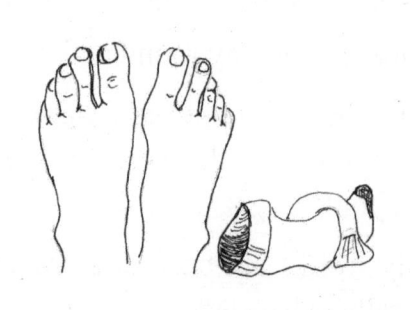

A meal at Carol's but everyone soon realises I need to be back in bed so Ted walks me back (2 chalets away) I zonk again until 5 o'clock in the morning. Getting up I have several mugs of tea and go for a walk on the coastal path, summer is still with us, it is a beautiful morning, I sit on my spot where I ponder and dream, my special place where I have watched many beautiful sunsets, and felt on top of the world.

I am very lucky I had no injuries or pain, I feel what shall I say, a bit limp. At this stage it is my head that is causing concern, it feels like cotton wool, all the concentration I suppose, this lasted for about a week, thankfully returning back to normal. Hang on Rosie be truthful about your story, there is nothing 'normal' about you.....

ON REFLECTION

On reflection there were areas where I was totally unprepared.

On reflection it had never occurred to me to pace my walk, all I could think about was getting to my next 'pit stop' without injury and making mistakes. I am very clumsy and have no sense of direction (good job I was walking ROUND AN ISLAND). Totally believing that the places I wasn't familiar with I would 'remember' from my practice walks, yeah, yeah, easy, I can remember that bit!! Well actually no, I couldn't.

On reflection another mistake I made, Carol asked me beforehand

'Did you do some night walking Rosie? I replied with a nervous laugh. Hmm, well, actually no I truly never gave it a thought.

On reflection, night walking was a big learning curve, apart from stating the obvious, fields seem twice as long, twice as wide, paths are longer, descents are deeper, ascents are steeper. Trees and bushes look very menacing in the night sky. Torch beams make everywhere look spooky, lighting up tree roots, rocks, pot holes. One slip, a sprained ankle or worse.

On reflection another surprise the amount of food I consumed, well what a gannet, bacon, eggs, ham rolls, cheese, bananas and KitKats by the handful. Had it not been for Peter's nagging with food and drink I'm pretty sure I would have collapsed through lack of nourishment.

On reflection Rosie remember the sea goes in and out, something called the tide!!

On reflection an organised walk is vastly different to going out on your 'Jack Jones', no signs directing the way, no water stations, no marshals in hi vis jackets, egging you on with a big smile, and last but not least, NO ST JOHN'S AMBULANCE …...JUST IN CASE!!

On a big reflection I went through every emotion you can think of, from the depths of despair to being sky high, and all the in betweens, happy, sad, angry, impatient, tantrums, tears, excitement, to name but a few.

MY THANKS

My thanks to my team of supporters without them I couldn't have done it. I think Peter had just as much of an ordeal as me, to sit and wait for me at every pit stop, to judge my mood as to whether he gave comfort or shouted, for him to be deprived of sleep also, hmm, not easy.

My thanks to Carol and Ted, who returned to the island just to help, little did they know what their involvement would be. I hasten to add we are still friends…...

Thank you Carol for volunteering Ted, bless you Ted you were a star, so unprepared, but you achieved, that's man power for you.

My thanks to Bill, the apparition at the bathroom window, walking that bad tempered, ungrateful, smelly woman from Cowes to Gurnard.

A big thank you to my boss and friend in the hospice, Jillian, for giving me an amazing massage on the Monday, much, much needed.

And of course a very, very big thank you to all who put money into my pot for our island hospice.

Well done to everyone

ROSIE

WHERE THE MONEY WENT

Pots, plates, trinket dishes, piggy banks, mugs etc to name but a few.

Being a volunteer doing hand massage and nails I often drifted into the art room when I wasn't busy

So many creative patients eager to do different things.

Chatting with Katie who ran things and a genius at 'thinking up something new' asked

me if she could buy a kiln with the monies raised, well the whole room went into a frenzy.

Julie, who gave me a hug at the chain ferry, had been fundraising at the same time, used her money to buy blank pottery and paints.

Once it was all set up, patients, family, even staff were all 'at it' creating their master pieces.

It was pure joy to see so many people getting so much enjoyment, a rewarding and

fore filling end result of my slog.

Alas I think after about seven years the kiln 'conked out' with much use and numerous

repairs ……..

Thank you Katie for all your hard work.

Rosie x

ANNE HOLLEY

Born in 1951 I spent my school years in Mortlake Middlesex.

Moving to Shepperton with my family at the age of 14.

I worked my apprenticeship as a hairdresser.

I have two children, four grandchildren and two great granddaughters.

Now retired my hobbies are walking, dancing and writing for charity.

Two books by Anne Holley

ALICE WHERE ARE YOU

Alice, who is a Cavalier King Charles Spaniel, is the narrator of my book, so I lived inside her head for eighteen months hmm….

The border collies also have voices with their very own different personalities again hmm….

'Now I've rounded up all the sheep does that mean I am a border collie' gasps Alice.

The moans and groans from two humans and four border collies say it all.

All profits from my books go to
Admiral Nurses UK.
Thank you, Anne Holley

WHY AM I DOING THIS

This lovely, humorous, little book tells the stories of Rosie's exploits as an intrepid fundraiser, ranging from dressing dolls to abseiling down the Spinnaker Tower, and trekking into and out of the Grand Canyon.

All profits from my books go to
Admiral Nurses UK.
Thank you, Anne Holley

Milton Keynes UK
Ingram Content Group UK Ltd.
UKHW051446181123
432786UK00010B/19

9 781803 699523